THE
Archive Photographs
SERIES

PORTH AND RHONDDA FACH

Promotional photograph for Howells department store in Cardiff taken at Lewis Merthyr Colliery in 1973.

THE
Archive Photographs
SERIES
PORTH AND RHONDDA FACH

Compiled by
Aldo Bacchetta and Glyn Rudd

CHALFORD

First published 1996
Copyright © Aldo Bacchetta and Glyn Rudd, 1996

The Chalford Publishing Company
St Mary's Mill, Chalford,
Stroud, Gloucestershire, GL6 8NX

ISBN 0 7524 0694 9

Typesetting and origination by
The Chalford Publishing Company
Printed in Great Britain by
Redwood Books, Trowbridge

Also published in the *Archive Photographs* series:

Rhondda (Simon Eckley and Emrys Jenkins)
Rhondda: A Second Selection (Simon Eckley and Emrys Jenkins)

Group of blacksmiths from the Lewis Merthyr Colliery, *c.* 1935.

Contents

Rhys Bevan Jones. Born in Dowlais on 19 September 1869, he was ordained in 1893. After a number of pastorates he came to Salem chapel, Porth then to Ainon chapel, Ynyshir. During this time he formed the South Wales Bible Institute at Tynycymmer Hall, Porth which ran from 1916 to 1936. On 28 September 1919, Rhys Bevan Jones began his ministry at Tabernacle chapel, Porth. After thirteen and a half years as pastor there he became seriously ill with a brain tumour and died in April 1933. He was buried at Trealaw Cemetery.

Pastor Rhys Bevan Jones' Bible Institute at Tynycymmer Hall, Porth, 1920s.

HIRAETH

'Hiraeth' is a special word,
Translation is denied;
So many deep emotions,
To this word can be applied.

It's longing for our mountains
And a thousand crystal streams,
The valleys and the meadows
That are always in our dreams.

We miss the 'Hymns and Arias'
The balm of every grief,
The songs of celebrations,
That strengthens our belief.

It's a yearning for our Home-land,
With a love that never fails,
And it's only known to Welsh-folk
For it was made in Wales.

(Poem reproduced courtesy of Les Harries, Faversham, Kent)

Foreword

Those of us who have been privileged to grow up in the Rhondda Valley are fortunate people. We have been the inheritors of a fierce pride in our community because of the tumultuous fight for human rights, which characterised our mining community in the closing years of the nineteenth century and throughout the twentieth century.

We are the children of giants. Our forebears had moral and physical courage on a limitless scale. They had high standards because they had unwavering faith in the brotherhood of mankind. The nobility of their bearing was revealed in their firm conviction that we are our brothers' keepers. We are responsible for caring for the whole community.

For these reasons I am grateful to Mr Glyn Rudd and Mr Aldo Bacchetta for their joint decision to write a book on Porth and Rhondda Fach. They are the right people to undertake this task because they belong to the community. Their stories spring from their own experiences and from their vivid memories. Such books as this remind us of Rhondda's mighty history.

I am proud to write this foreword for I love our two valleys dearly.

George Thomas
Right Honourable The Viscount Tonypandy PC, (Hon) DCL
Speaker, House of Commons 1976-1983

The Revd Rex McPherson

Introduction

We love the people, but would gladly trade the weather! This is our response to people who ask us how we like living in Wales. Even after being in the country for seven and one half years, we STILL LOVE the PEOPLE and still would trade the weather!

Coming to Wales from America in 1989, we found a culture that was much different from our own. Everything was an adjustment for us, from driving to buying food. At first, we found it difficult, but with the help of some very kind and gracious people at Bethany Baptist church in Ynyshir, Rhondda Fach, we settled in rather quickly.

As a preacher of the Gospel of Christ, I was called of God to serve Him in this land of beauty. My wife, Jessica, and daughter, Christine, and I have travelled throughout the Principality, not only viewing the landscape but also meeting the people. In all of Wales, the Rhondda Fach is like NO OTHER PLACE. The valley flows with a river of people from Maerdy at the top to Porth, the gateway to the Rhondda. This valley is not long nor is it wide. The black gold that once drew people from far and wide no longer fires the hearths of most dwellings, but that same treasure from the earth has left behind a treasure of greater worth – the people of the Rhondda Fach.

Through adversity, toil, hardship and Christian revival, a people of unique character and quality has come forth as a shining gemstone. The Rhondda Fach is often called the forgotten valley, but I can truly say that God has not forgotten her and never will for He still loves her people with the sacrificing love of Calvary. Nor will this preacher and his family ever forget their time of ministry in the Rhondda Fach.

Revd Kenneth Rex McPherson, Pastor of Bethany Baptist church
Ynyshir, Porth, Rhondda, 14 July 1996

One

Porth, Cymmer and Trehafod

'The Gateway to the Rhondda' – Porth railway station as it was c. 1914.

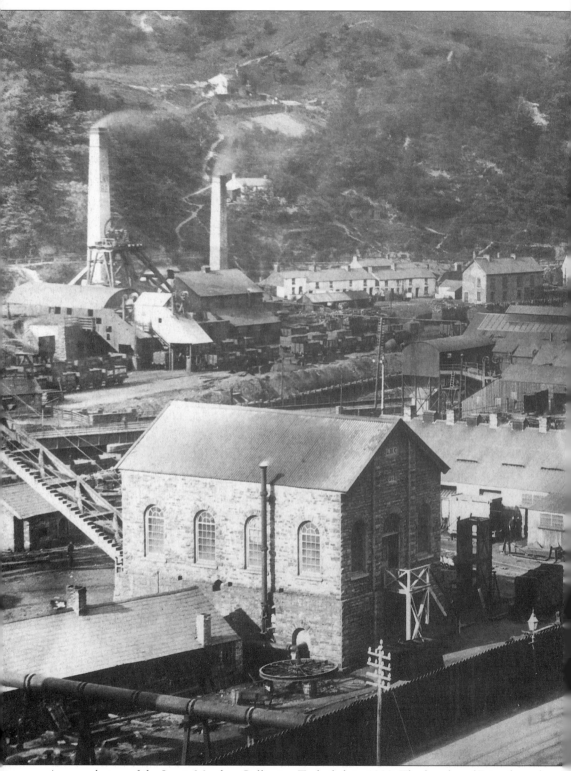

A general view of the Lewis Merthyr Collieries, Trehafod, in 1900. The hamlet of Fairoak, and

Cwm George, can be seen in the background.

A group of ponies used at the Lewis Merthyr Collieries at the turn of the century. The white one on the left was named 'Snowball'.

The Lewis Merthyr Colliery Band in 1950, with their conductor, Oliver Jones.

'Where's everyone gone?' Mr Glyn Harris stands in the yard of Lewis Merthyr Colliery on the day it closed (14 March 1983).

Lewis Merthyr miners celebrating their pools win in the York Hotel, Porth, 1950s.

Lewis Merthyr Colliery outing to Worcester Races, 1952.

Group of Lewis Merthyr Colliery
blacksmiths and maintenance men, 1942.

General view of Britannia, Porth in 1910. The building in the foreground is the Britannia Hotel
now known as 'The Lodge'.

The new Eirw Road Bridge, which was opened in 1910 to connect Britannia with Porth. The building on the left is the old fire station, now S. & F. Motors.

This Dennis fire engine was presented by the Rhondda Urban District Council to the Porth Fire Brigade on 18 May 1929. William Evans JP can be seen (left) in the act of christening the vehicle the *Lady Rhondda*.

One of George Insole's pits at Cymmer, Porth, 1880s, a site occupied today by the Pioneer supermarket. George Insole and his son, coal dealers from Cardiff, took a lease on 375 acres of land at Cymmer, Porth on 25 September 1844. This lease was to run for a period of seventy years, for the purposes of extracting coal from the South Cymmer Level. In 1847 Insole sunk his first pit (pictured above) and found fine coking coal. By the following year thirty-six coke ovens had also been erected. By 1851 the Upper Cymmer Colliery had been sunk and four years later in 1855 the New Cymmer Colliery was opened. From 1860 to 1889 this new colliery was to be leased to T.C. Hinde. Two more shafts were to be sunk on Cymmer Yard, work commencing in 1875 and completed in 1877. Coal was mined at Cymmer until 1940 when all work stopped and the collieries closed.

CYMMER EXPLOSION

On 15 July 1856 an explosion took place at Cymmer Colliery. At the time 160 men and boys were underground. At first, it was feared that all had lost their lives but by some miracle 46 had survived. It was not until the evening of the 16th that the number of lives lost could be accurately calculated – 114 men and boys. At the Coroner's inquest it was said that the manager of the colliery, Mr Jabez Thomas, seldom went underground, his chief occupation being the attending of the disposal of the coal at the surface. The overman and fireman took charge of the underground workings under the direction of the above ground manager (i.e. Mr Thomas). Witnesses at the inquest stated that the mine had been in a dangerous state and that the indication of firedamp had been observed for some time before the accident. The coroner's jury, after a long and patient hearing, returned a verdict of manslaughter against Jabez Thomas, manager; Rowland Rowland, overman and three firemen. However, at the assizes held at Swansea, the Judge, Mr Baron Watson, in his address to the jury, said that in as much as Mr Jabez Thomas was the above ground Manager and did not go underground, he could not be held responsible and as regards the other men, no direct case of omission was brought against them and he could not see how they could be guilty of manslaughter. All five accused were eventually acquitted.

Cymmer Colliery as it was in 1920 and below as it appears today with the site occupied by the Pioneer supermarket and car park.

Y Gapel, High Street, Cymmer, built in 1870. Seen here in 1938, it was known locally as 'Ty Cwrdd Splits'.

Yr Hen Gapel. This is the oldest Nonconformist chapel in Rhondda (1738) and there are plans for it to be dismantled and re-erected at the Rhondda Heritage Park.

'Nyth-brân House' where Guto Nyth-brân (Griffith Morgan) lived. Legend has it that when the valleys from Blaenrhondda and Maerdy were heavily wooded it happened that two squirrels started from respective points in the 'Fach' and 'Fawr' on their daily hop to Pontypridd. They met at the apex – Porth – and started to race. Whether their activity was an inspiration for 'Guto Nyth-brân' is not clearly known, but what is certain is that his amazing feats as a runner started a tradition of sporting prowess of which Porth can be well proud.

Guto was a shepherd on Nyth-brân mountain in the early part of the eighteenth century, and the story goes that his speed and endurance were developed by daily chasing of fractious sheep. Whatever the training, he became proudly proclaimed by the 'Snakes' of Aberdare, the 'Glorans' of the Rhonddas, and the 'Black Pirates' of Llantrisant as Wales' fleetest runner.

Those were not the days of 'state of the art' tracks, scientific preparations, or even spiked shoes and stringed paths. Guto, instead, ran mostly in bare feet. Once, he defeated by many hundreds of yards a fast horse over ten miles of ground, but the herculean tasks, in the way of handicaps, ultimately killed him, one of the most tragic deaths in the history of sport.

On his tombstone in St Gwynno's churchyard, Llanwynno, it is recorded that Guto covered a measured twelve miles of mountain ground in seven minutes within the hour! His sweetheart was among the supporters who wagered heavily on him on this his final race, for which he gave an 'out of sight' start to his opponent. Knowing him to be running in bare feet some scheming gambler scattered broken glass on the floor of a bridge that had to be crossed en route. When he arrived at the spot, however, Nyth-brân spotted the danger and leapt onto and ran along the parapet thus avoiding the glass. Despite this act of sabotage and the serious 'handicap' Guto caught his opponent within a few yards of the tape. So delighted was his sweetheart with this success that she ran up to him and clapped him heavily on the back. He started violently and fell to the ground. Turning agonized eyes upon her, he explained, 'Dyna ti wedi fy lladd i' ('There, you have killed me'), and died on the spot.

Unemployed men repairing shoes in Porth House, 1920s. Cecil Edward Briffet is second from the right in the front.

Group of musicians from Glyn Street, Porth, 1933. Arthur Hopkins is on mouth-organ in the second row.

Percy Jones met Eugene Criqui on 26 March 1914 at Liverpool Stadium as America had up to then not recognised the flyweight of 8 stone. Eugene Criqui of France, was the recognised champion on the Continent, and had beaten Jones once on points. In the meantime, Percy, in one of the greatest flyweight bouts of all time, had beaten Bill Ladbury at the National Sporting Club for the Lonsdale Belt, and when Criqui and Jones were matched in the return it was described in all reputable newspapers, as well as the sporting papers, as for 'the world's flyweight title.' The Americans did not attempt to question this, and when Percy won he held the right to this title.

Porth Square in 1888. The large building in the centre-right of the photograph was Dr Naunton Davies' house. At the front can be seen the first lump of coal mined at Cymmer Colliery. During the 1926 Miners' Strike it was broken up and distributed to the needy. The three-storey building to the left is Capel-y-Porth. Below: the same scene 65 years later in 1953.

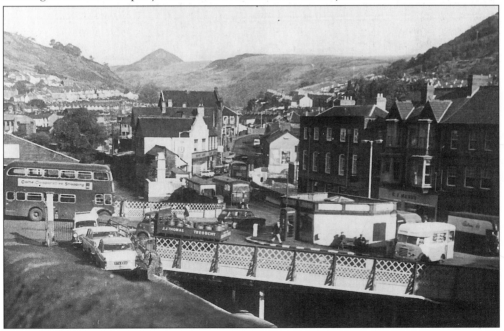

Forty-seven people released from Cymmer set up an independent chapel (Capel y Porth) with the support of D. Thomas and T. George in 1879. Seven deacons were selected and Idris Williams played a leading role in the chapel's development (he was also a lay preacher). The chapel initally met at the vestry of Capel-y-Trefnyddion but soon needed their own chapel and set about finding a site. The new chapel (above) opened on 30 or 31 May 1880. The cost was £2371 4s 6d. William Jones deputised for B. Davies several times before being appointed as minister early in 1881 and ordained in May that year.

Porth and District War Memorial which was erected on the bank of the River Rhondda in 1928 to commemorate the loss of life during the First World War.

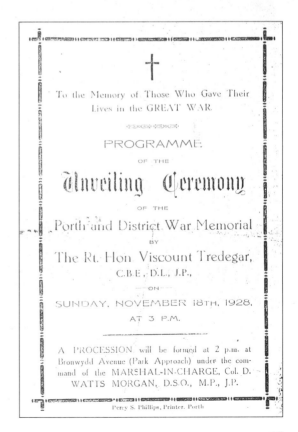

To the Memory of Those Who Gave Their Lives in the GREAT WAR.

PROGRAMME

OF THE

Unveiling Ceremony

OF THE

Porth and District War Memorial

BY

The Rt. Hon Viscount Tredegar,

C.B.E., D.L., J.P.,

ON

SUNDAY, NOVEMBER 18TH, 1928,

AT 3 P.M.

A PROCESSION will be formed at 2 p.m. at Bronwydd Avenue (Park Approach) under the command of the MARSHAL-IN-CHARGE, Col. D. WATTS MORGAN, D.S.O., M.P., J.P.

Percy S. Phillips, Printer, Porth

The front cover of the programme for the unveiling ceremony, 18 November 1928.

Opening of the new head post office, Porth Square, 5 October 1925. From left to right: Councillor John Morgans (Chairman, Porth and District Chamber of Trade); Lieut. Col. D. Watts Morgan MP, CBE, DSO, JP; Lieut. Col. F.H. Kempe MC (Surveyor, GPO); Mr D.W. Hughes (Head Postmaster); Councillor William Evans JP (President, Porth and District Chamber of Trade); Mr A.J. Williams (Hon. Secretary, Porth and District Chamber of Trade).

Memorial to William Evans JP (1864-1934), joint founder of Thomas & Evans and the 'Corona pop' business. He donated Bronwydd Park to the people of Porth.

Bronwydd House, home of William Evans. It was designed for him by a French architect in the 1920s. It is now council offices.

Bronwydd (Porth) Park swimming baths in the 1930s.

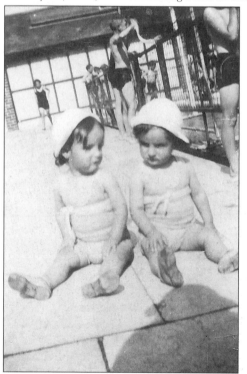

Left: twins Mario and Aldo Bacchetta at Bronwydd swimming baths in 1938. Right: Anthea Davies, with son Mark, at Porth Park in 1963.

Thomas & Evans' emergency food transport staff, including the regular 'Bread Brigade', during the Railway Strike in 1926. William Evans is pictured in the inset.

Just a line from Barry Island

Porth and Rhondda Fach miners on holiday at Barry Island, 1931. The 'miners' fortnight' – the annual two-week summer break from the collieries – saw South Wales coastal resorts such as Barry Island and Porthcawl packed by the men and their extended families. Note the little girl (left) who looks none too comfortable on her placid mount.

Welsh Guards' dance at the Rink, North Road, Porth, *c.* 1935. Included in this picture, with other dignitaries and guests, are Lieut. Col. D. Watts Morgan MP, CBE, DSO, JP, Mrs Louisa

Luckwell (seated first right on floor) and her father, Edward Mewett (first on left of picture).

'Young Rhondda Bucks Night Out at the Rink Ballroom, Porth', 1949. Among those pictured:
T. Williams, H. Barrow, H. May, B. Bateman, R. Bacchetta, M. Williams, Viv Rees, K. Powell.

Murray Williams' School of Dancing, Bethania chapel, North Road, Porth, 1950s.

Street party in Eirw Road, Britannia, Porth to celebrating the coronation of Queen Elizabeth II in 1953.

Concert performed by members of Sion Welsh Baptist chapel, Birchgrove, Porth, 1950s.

Juniors at Llwyncelyn School in 1953.

Lilian Evans of Porth pictured with Hughie Green (left) when he visited Steinbergs, Treforest in 1950.

Standard 6 at Porth Council Girls' School in 1913.

Standard II at Porth Boys' School in 1928.

TOWN HALL, Porth.

Three Nights Only .... Commencing MONDAY, AUGUST 13th, 1894.

HARDIE & VON LEER'S

Superb

Scenic

Production

OF

L. J. Carter's

Great

Play,

THE FLIGHT OF THE FAST MAIL

The FAST MAIL.

David Allen & Sons, Belfast, London, Manchester, and New York.

With all

its

Marvellous

Scenic

AND

Mechanical

Effects.

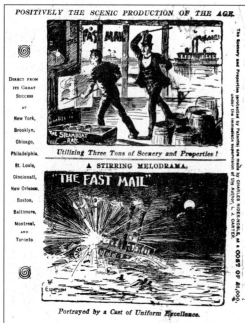

POSITIVELY THE SCENIC PRODUCTION OF THE AGE.

DIRECT FROM ITS GREAT SUCCESS AT New York, Brooklyn, Chicago, Philadelphia, St. Louis, Cincinnati, New Orleans, Boston, Baltimore, Montreal, AND Toronto.

Utilizing Three Tons of Scenery and Properties!

A STIRRING MELODRAMA.

"THE FAST MAIL"

Portrayed by a Cast of Uniform Excellence.

The Scenery and Properties produced by Pilberto, are made by CHARLES RIDER-NOBLE, at a COST OF £1,000, under the immediate supervision of the Author, L. J. CARTER.

COMEDY, FUN, INTEREST, and WONDER GO HAND-IN-HAND.

See the Practical Working Locomotive, DRAWING FOURTEEN FULL-SIZED FREIGHT CARS.

A Ponderous Train 280 ft. long and 12 ft. high, and

⋇ THE FLIGHT OF "THE FAST MAIL" ⋇

Taking up the "Mail" at 40 miles an hour.

THE GREATEST STAGE EFFECTS EVER PRODUCED

Every Scene and Property used in the production of this successful play is carried by the Company, and will be positively shown at Every Performance exactly as advertised.

THE FAST MAIL

This realistic melodrama is now being played by Five Companies! Three in America, and Two in England, Nightly Entertaining Thousands of Delighted Spectators.

NOT A DULL MOMENT IN THE PLAY!

THOUSANDS ARE SORRY THEY DID NOT SEE THE FAST MAIL

DON'T YOU BE ONE OF THEM.

'The Good Old Days'. Before the arrival of the silent movie, live performances entertained packed audiences in the Town Hall. This particular one was on a world tour and would have been the first of its kind to be seen in the Rhondda. The stage effects were electrifying and kept everyone in a state of total amazement and laughter.

A STUPENDOUS REALIZATION OF

NIAGARA FALLS

AS ACTUALLY PRODUCED IN

Hardie & Von Leer's

SUPERB SCENIC PRODUCTION OF L. J. CARTER'S GREAT PLAY

With its

Roaring Cataract

Rising Mist,

Rainbow Effects,

&c.

THE FAST MAIL

Without doubt the

Most Realistic

and

Ponderous Scene

ever placed on

any Stage.

100—NOVEL FEATURES NEVER BEFORE ATTEMPTED—100.

FRANK A. GORDYN and HALDANE CRICHTON, Managers.

Mr Townsend, manager, and staff of the Central Cinema, Porth, late 1930s. This building is now the Palladium bingo hall.

Miss Williams pictured outside her father's tobacconist shop in 1904. She was to become the mother of Roy Thomas who has the fancy goods shop in Hannah Street, Porth.

Hannah Street, Porth, *c.* 1905.

Lewis, Milliners and Drapers, 59 Hannah Street, Porth, 1910.

'Express Delivery Service of Silent Movies' to the Central Cinema, Porth (i.e. the man walking towards the camera), Hannah Street, c. 1920.

'Father Christmas' outside Thomas & Evans, Hannah Street, Porth, 1956.

Dimambro's Café and Tobacconist, Pontypridd Road, Porth, 1921. This is now the site of Porth Library.

Hannah Street, Porth, decorated in preparation for the visit of King George V and Queen Mary to the Rhondda in 1912.

View of Hannah Street from Barclays Bank (card postmarked 1948).

Hannah Street, Porth, *c.* 1925. On the left is the Primitive Methodist chapel.

Llwyncelyn ladies versus gents football match played with one hand tied behind the back. Such entertainment helped alleviate the boredom and misery of the 1926 Strike.

Not a great deal has changed since this picture of Tynewydd Square, Porth was taken some seventy years ago.

First tram to leave for Ferndale from the Rhondda Tramways Company's depot at Porth, 1908.

43

Rhondda Tramways' staff, c. 1910. From left to right, on the tram: Les Williams, Ozzie Martin. In front of tram: Frank Gill, W. Jack, Alf Bully and George Jones.

Rhondda Tramways' employees at Shand's, Porthcawl in 1933 for the annual 'poor children's outing'. Mr and Mrs Tom Hanley and family are seated front left of picture.

The Rhondda Tramways AFC, 1924-25 season.

Rhondda Transport Rugby Football Club, before a match against AEC Southall in 1956. Among those pictured are Don May, Howard May, Ron Bacchetta, G. Wells, G. Lloyd, T. Owen, J. Nicholas.

Rhondda Transport football team, 1959. Among those pictured are: Bill Anthony, Jack Bower, Mr Scott (Chief Engineer), Mr Chapman, Len Williams, Bill Herbert, Steve Norris, Tommy Ashford, Lyn Evans, Geoff Evans, 'Driver' Pugh, Ray Pope, John Norris, Geoff Howells.

The Cottage Hospital, Porth, c. 1910. On 17 October 1994 Porth Hospital celebrated one hundred years of service to the people of the Rhondda Valleys. Major accidents, such as the Tynewydd Colliery disaster at Cymmer in April 1877, made it clear to miners and doctors that there was a shocking lack of surgical and medical facilities in the coalfield. The five men who were rescued from their underground tomb after nine days, had to be cared for in a makeshift fashion in a room at the Tynewydd Hotel, Porth. Until the emergence of hospitals, injuries underground were dealt with on the spot, in the home, or in the doctor's consulting room. The slow improvement of facilities in Rhondda began with the building of Ystradyfodwg Cottage Hospital at Tyntyla in 1887. When this hospital was taken over by the Rhondda Urban District Council in 1897, the number of beds increased from four to ten in order to cater for the treatment of infectious diseases. In 1902 a new building, known as Tyntyla Isolation Hospital, was built on adjoining land and provided thirty-two beds in two pavilions. Similarly, in 1908 the District Council completed the erection of a smallpox hospital on top of Penrhys mountain, providing beds for twenty patients. This was hardly adequate for the booming population of Rhondda which then stood at about 120,000, particularly if one considers that no other hospitals were built or subsidized by the local authorities before 1914. Fortunately for Porth and district, a Cottage Hospital had opened in 1894 as a result of miners' subscriptions and the work of benefactors such as Dr Henry Naunton Davies, who had led the team of nine medical men during the Tynewydd Colliery disaster. He lived and practised in Porth where he became surgeon to eleven collieries and works, a Ministry of Health Certified Factory Surgeon and Public Vaccinator. A plaque commemorating his contribution to the founding of the hospital is still there and the ward named after him is now the operating theatre suite. Porth Cottage Hospital helped to fill the void in the community's health and welfare service. With the high incidence of ill-health, there was a great need for medical treatment. However, in the days before the National Health Service, the cost had to be borne by the patient and it was often those who were ill or injured who could least afford to pay. Working conditions in the collieries at the time were appalling, safety conditions were non-existent and accidents occurred with depressing regularity. While both the government and the mine-owners shirked responsibility for welfare provision, it was left largely to the miners themselves to build the hospitals in the Rhondda. Through weekly contributions and annual charity events, they were able to greatly improve the medical facilities.

'Empire Week' Carnival Queen, pictured here with nurses and staff outside Porth Cottage Hospital, 1920s.

Staff Nurse Mair Jones after passing her 'State Registered Nurse' examination at Porth Hospital in 1952.

Porth Secondary Grammar School, 1944-45. Among those pictured: Vivian John, Idwal Clarke, John Jones, Keith Noakes, Ron Bacchetta, John Richards, Kenny Young, Selwyn Jenkins, Hugh Barron, Mair Head, Dorothy Grundy, Sylvia Edmunds, Valmai Davies, Graham Webster, Alan Williams, Joyce Davies, Mari Lewis, Ann Morgan.

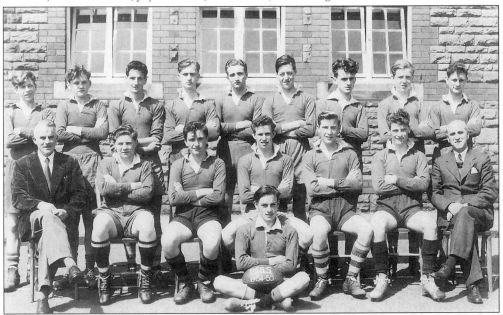

Porth Secondary Grammar School rugby first-team, 1954-55 season with headmaster, Mr Emlyn Morgan and sports master, Mr Emrys James. Among the boys pictured: Norman Carter, Brian Griffiths, Mario Bacchetta, Mike Bent, Gwyn Williams, Ray Cheynne, Alun Williams, Gareth Jones, Ralph Williams, Cliff Evans, Gerald Long, Roy Weekes.

Standard 3 at Llwyncelyn School, late 1940s.

A decorated bike at the 1910 Porth Carnival.

Checking and preparing gas masks at Islwyn School, Mount Pleasant, Porth in 1939.

Teachers and parents boxing and distributing gas masks at Islwyn School, Mount Pleasant, Porth, 1939. On the right of picture is Mrs Louisa Luckwell.

No 1 Platoon, 'B' Company, Porth Home Guard, 1940.

Porth Army Cadets, 1943. Among those pictured are: Arthur Rees, H. Packer, Clarence Francis, Ormond Thomas, Eddie England, Major Bob Pugh, Don May, Stewart Peters.

Evacuees pictured with the children of Birchgrove, Porth, 1941.

Two Rhondda boys (Ptes Crowther and Wilfred Jones of Wattstown) serving in Ireland, 1940.

Warrant Officer Jenkin Thomas Williams, Porth, December 1942. He was wireless operator and an air gunner during the Second World War.

3rd Platoon, 'B' Company, Trebanog, Porth Home Guard, 1940.

Llwyncelyn Home Guard, 1940.

Servants of law and order: Special Constabulary attached to Porth Police Station in 1940.

Infantry men leaving a landing-craft on the beach at Anzio in January 1944 during the Allied invasion of Italy in the Second World War. Right foreground of the picture is Emlyn Bibey of Cymmer, Porth.

Porth Civil Defence, 1950s.

DON'T GO DOWN THE MINE, DAD. (1)

A miner was leaving his home for his work,
When he heard his little child scream;
He went to his bedside, his little white face,
"Oh Daddy, I've had such a dream
I dreamt that I saw the pit all afire,
And men struggled hard for their lives;
The scene it then changed, and the top of the mine
Was surrounded by sweethearts and wives"

WORDS BY PERMISSION OF THE LAWRENCE WRIGHT MUSIC CO.
29, CONDUIT STREET, LEICESTER.

MEMORIES OF PORTH (DILWYN EVANS)

On the following four pages are edited extracts of conversations with Mr Dilwyn Evans of Porth. They provide a picture of Rhondda life that will be familiar to the many thousands of men and women who suffered and survived the experience of the 1920s and 1930s.

UNEMPLOYMENT AND THE MEANS TEST

After living in apartments for so long, my parents managed to get a house in Aldergrove Road. After leaving the Royal Air Force my father found work as an 'ostler' looking after the pit ponies in Cymmer Colliery. This work continued until he was put out of work after the 1926 strike and apart from short periods of temporary work he did not find full-time employment until he went to Coventry in 1937. Life was hard in those days. There were no family allowances. Social security as we know it now did not exist. During the years of unemployment my father did manage to obtain temporary spells of work as a relieving officer but that did not help him when he sometimes applied for poor relief. I remember how when he applied the relieving officer would come to the house to assess our family's needs and we would be told to sell an item of furniture to obtain more money. At the end the only piece of furniture left in the parlour was a piano. The only way that my mother was able to keep it was to say that it belonged to her mother. Such was the dreaded means test of the day.

The house we lived in at Aldergrove Road was in a terrace of approximately nine houses. They were flat-fronted with no garden in the front. With the exception of one family (the Mainwarings) all the others were unemployed men. On the opposite side of the road were the 'posh' houses, with bay windows, gardens in the front and all were occupied by professional people: Mr Davies, headmaster of Porth Secondary School; Mr Howells, retired headmaster of Iswlyn School, Mr Davies, the bank manager, to name just a few. Mrs Davies (the Bank) used to pass items of clothing, etc., to my mother and once she gave a pair of Mr Davies' old brown shoes. They fitted me and what a toff I felt with them! Over the years I have never forgotten my first pair of brown shoes.

DON'T GO DOWN THE MINE, DAD (No. 2).
"Don't go down in the mine, Dad,
Dreams very often come true;
Daddy, you know it would break my heart.
If anything happened to you;
Just go and tell my dream to your mates,
And as true as the stars that shine,
Something is going to happen to-day,
Dear Daddy, don't go down the mine!"

SCHOOLDAYS, THE BEST DAYS?

My schooldays were spent in Islwyn School and I well remember some of the teachers: Mr Tal Lewis, Mr Williams (his parents kept a newsagent's shop in Pontypridd Road) and Mr Griffiths, but the one who stands uppermost in my mind is Mr Emrys Jenkins. He taught us in all subjects, including a short course in shorthand and simple book-binding. I can remember vividly how he instructed the boys to make a garden. This was made in the school grounds. Adjacent to the school were allotments and in the corner were the boys' toilets to which we had to go no matter what the weather conditions were. In a patch in front of the toilets we made the garden. We grew flowers, vegetables and even made a goldfish pond out of a large galvanized square tank which was sunk into the ground. A pipe was laid from the toilets in order to make a fountain. As far as I was concerned Mr Jenkins has been my mentor all my grown life.

On one occasion my sister Teify did not attend school due to illness and I was asked to go and see her teacher. On the way to her classroom I mumbled to myself, not being heard so I thought, that her teacher (Miss Smith) was a 'bloody nuisance'. The girl who had come for me reported me to the teacher. Consequently, I was sent for by Mr Lloyd, the headmaster. After giving me a lecture on the error of my ways he gave me six of the best on each hand. I wondered what would have happened had that been today, but one thing I can assure you of is that I never swore again. Even so, I never told my father about it because he would have given me six more strokes. To rub salt in the wound we were sent by teachers to a local shop to purchase the cane which administered the punishment!

At the age of about 11, I went to a school in Ynyshir to sit the examination for secondary school. I passed the exam for Porth County School but due to my parents' financial situation I could not go. At that time, 'Boppa Rees' who lived with us, told my mother that if her eldest son Maldwyn ever passed she would 'by hook or by crook' let him go. When visiting Porth a few years ago I met Raymond Rees, Maldwyn's brother (Maldwyn had unfortunately drowned in the sea off Penarth). Raymond told me that the same thing had happened to Maldwyn who passed the exam for Porth Secondary School, only to be withdrawn because his parents could not afford to keep him there.

Sunday was always given to church going, three times, morning and evening with my parents' brother and sisters, then Sunday schools in the afternoon. After church on Sunday evening in the summer we would go for a walk along the back of the houses in Cemetery Road, along the foot of the mountain, through a farmyard and come out on Trealaw Road and then return home.

When I was in my early teens I was allowed to go out on my own. In those days the most popular place on Sunday evening was Hannah Street where the boys walked on one side, the girls on the other, until we reached the end of the street where we crossed over and went back on the other side. There is a saying that marriages are made in heaven but I wonder how many started in Hannah Street.

The first bicycle I ever had was a unique model being a genuine ASP (all spare parts!) and cost two shillings. It was built by the Ashford Brothers in Charles Street. I well remember the number of times I went over the handle bars when the front wheel got stuck in the tram lines by the Tynewydd Hotel. The lines crossed and converged on each other there, one set going up the Rhondda Fawr to Treherbert, one set going up the Rhondda Fach to Maerdy and the other going in to the old tram depot. On one corner was Dan Jones' fruit store, next to which was his house. In the 1930s the front door was always open so that everyone who passed could admire the international caps of his son, Cliff, who in those days was called 'the Wizard of Welsh Rugby Football'.

The highlight of the year was Christmas and New Years' Day. On Christmas Day my parents always bought us presents, perhaps a tin-plate clockwork train set or crayons and a colouring book. Looking back on how much money they had to spend they must have gone without themselves for us children. On New Years' Day it was the custom to call on local shopkeepers to wish them 'a happy New Year' and to receive a gift in return – Dan Jones, for example for the apple, orange and monkey nuts. We used to have our wrists stamped there, the idea being you did not queue a second time. Needless to say the stamp was soon rubbed off! Gambarini's, meanwhile, always gave a few sweets and a bar of chocolate and at the printer's shop at the top of the hill by the police station we used to get a pencil, ruler and writing book. That shop was where the old Porth Gazette was printed and is now a solicitor's office.

DON'T GO DOWN THE MINE, DAD. (3)

The miner, a man with a heart good and kind,
    Sat by the side of his son;
He said: "It's my living, I can't stay away,
    For duty, my lad, must be done."
The little one look'd up, and sadly he said:
    "Oh, please stay to-day with me, Dad!"
But as the brave miner went forth to his work,
    He heard this appeal from his lad –

WORDS BY PERMISSION OF THE LAWRENCE WRIGHT MUSIC CO.,
19, CONDUIT STREET, LEICESTER.

DON'T GO DOWN THE MINE, DAD. (4)

Whilst waiting his turn with his mates to descend
  He could not banish his fears,
He return'd home again to his wife and his child,
  Those words seem'd to ring through his ears.
And ere the day ended the pit was on fire,
  When a score of brave men lost their lives;
He thank'd God above for the dream his child had,
  As once more the little one cried:—

WORDS BY PERMISSION OF THE LAWRENCE WRIGHT MUSIC CO.
19, DENMARK STREET, LEICESTER.

As I grew older, the games became more adult – football and cricket. In those days we had our own 'Wembley Stadium'. It was bounded on one side by the river and we boys from the Aberrhondda had to cross by means of large stepping stones. Later, the Rhondda Council put what I think was a sewer pipe there. This was large in diameter and crossed the river at the right place to enable us to balance on it to get to the field. The lads from Charles Street had to cross the railway line which at that time was in use by trains. During the cricket season if we required a bat and stumps, these were bought for coppers from Jenkins' Timber Yard in Rheola Row.

In those days there were three cinemas in Porth: the Empire, Central and another which I cannot remember the name of, in Pontypridd Road opposite Hannah Street. The Empire was next to the Lewis Merthyr Library near Porth Square. Every Saturday morning the 'Penny Rush' was held there and Mrs Beynon, who managed it, used to patrol the aisle and if you got too noisy during the film she used to give you a crack on the head with a cane about ten feet long.

During our stay in Aldergrove the family increased and my sister Margaret and brother Cyril and David were born. When Margaret was born my mother had a very large green pram. This was kept for future use. When Cyril was born my pals and I used to take the youngsters for a walk, so my mother thought. What actually used to happen was that Margaret, who was about four, and Cyril, three years younger were put into the pram. We would take them to the hill by Terry's Stores and give them rides down the slope. I was at the stores and my pals someway down the hill. I would shout 'ready' and then let the pram go down the hill for my pals to catch it. What would have happened if they'd missed I now shudder to think.

At the age of 14½ I got work in the Lewis Merthyr Bertie Pit. How proud I felt to be the breadwinner in the family. Work in those days was hard, coal cutting being done by hand or be means of a compressed air drill. One of the men that I worked with had a Davy-lamp in addition to his electric one. I used to return the Davy-lamp to the lamp room and would turn my electric lamp off to show only the light of the oil lamp. Great visions used to pass through my mind of being the colliery manager walking in the mine roadway. My uncle Dai Griffiths worked on the afternoon shift and he would never go below ground until he had seen me and enquired if I was alright. I continued to work in the Bertie until October 1937 when my parents moved from the Rhondda to Coventry where my father had found work. On the 25 October 1937 I gave notice to leave the colliery and the then manager (Mr R. Rutherford) gave me a reference. (Reproduced courtesy of Mr Dilwyn Evans.)

Two
Ynyshir and Wattstown

General view of Ynyshir, 1990.

The Lady Lewis Colliery, Ynyshir *c*. 1906, while sinking was still in progress.

Mr Frankie Russell – who had been the last man to leave the Lady Lewis Colliery when it closed in 1926.

Jones Colliery, Ynyshir, sunk in 1849. Thomas Jones of Maindy House, Ynyshir bought the colliery in 1873. It closed around 1909.

Jones Colliery was sited on what is now the football field.

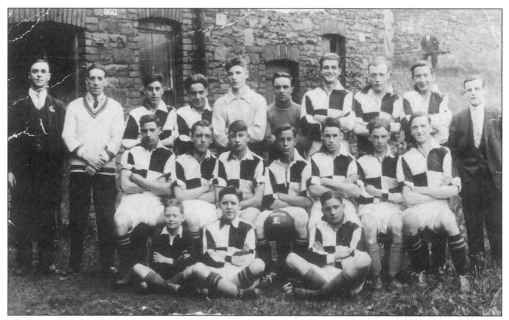

The Ynyshir Spartans football team in 1936, pictured at the back of the Eagle Hotel (now demolished).

Members of the Ynyshir Spartans Cricket Club, 1932.

Ynyshir Albion AFC, a most successful football team during the 1933-34 season. The trophies on display are the Wiltshire Cup, the Porth Hospital Cup (the Dr Orr Cup) and the Pontypridd League Championship Cup.

Ynyshir United AFC, 1947-48 season, winners of the Pontypridd and District League, 1946-47 and 1947-48. From left to right, back row: T. Bowen (Vice-Chairman), D. Jones, J.I. Evans (Assistant Secretary), C. Morgan, N. Stinton, E. Phelps. Middle row: A. Tanner (Trainer), W.J. Thomas, J. Pike, S. Kettley, D. Thomas, E. Franklin, G. Franklin, M. Kettley, E. Hughes, D. Edwards. Front row: G. Griffiths (Chairman), E. Williams, D. Phelps, G. Pooley, A. Adams (Captain), D. Serpell (Vice-Captain), T. Rees, J. Lewis, D. Roberts (Treasurer).

The men who sank the Standard Colliery, Ynyshir, *c.* 1876. Thomas Place, Ynyshir was built to accommodate these men and their families.

General view of Ynyshir in 1922. In the foreground is Penuel chapel. The pit in the background is the Standard Colliery.

Demolition of Penuel chapel, Ynyshir, August 1991.

Ynyshir Hall and Institute Cinema and the Station Hotel, c. 1920. Both these buildings were constructed in 1905.

Congregation of Ainon Welsh Baptist chapel, Ynyshir, celebrating their Silver Jubilee in 1909.

What remained of the Standard Colliery in 1950, at the top end of Ynyshir.

St Anne's church, Ynyshir, pictured before Heath Terrace was built, pre-1905.

Performers of the cantata, St Mary Magdalene Roman Catholic church, Ynyshir, 1937. This church later burned to the ground and a brand-new building was erected in its place.

Ainon Welsh Baptist Band of Hope, 1930. The conductress was Miss L. Jeanette Jones. Note that one of the band members was absent when the original photograph was taken. His slightly 'larger than life' face was added afterwards.

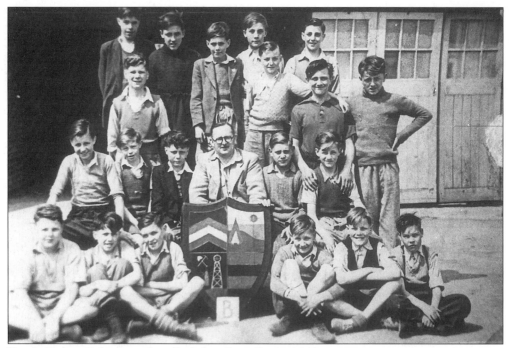

Ynyshir Junior School pupils at St Athan Boys Camp, 1948.

Standard IV at Ynyshir Junior Girls School, 1946.

Standard 2 at Ynyshir Junior School with Mr Gomer Evans, headmaster (left) and Miss Thomas, teacher, 1953.

Ynyshir Home Guard, 1940. In the background is all that was left of the disused Lady Lewis Colliery.

Ynyshir AFC, winners of the South Wales Shield, 1951.

The South Wales Shield being presented to Des Phelps by Mr Bundy, manager of Wattstown Colliery, 1951. Looking on (left) is Mr Jeff Craven.

Ynyshir Drum and Flute Band, 1926.

The newly-formed Ynyshir & Wattstown Junior Band, photographed at Wattstown Park in 1946.

Ynyshir Band with their conductor, G. Harris, taken on the lawn at Brynawel House, Ynyshir, 1960s. The band was first formed in 1946 under the direction of Captain Danny Liddell. Their first headquarters was the Old Band Room in the Station Hotel, Ynyshir where they stayed until the late 1970s. They then moved to the Co-operative Hall, which they had bought, spending a lot of time and money renovating the building. Recently the band was successful in applying to the Arts Council for Wales which administers National Lottery money for a grant, this money to be used for the administration of the band and band room.

Through the years they have won many awards including the National Mineworkers Brass Band Championship which was held in Blackpool in 1964 – the highest award that can be achieved. The band has a current membership of thirty seniors and twenty-three juniors, nearly fifty per cent of whom are girls, and there is always a welcome to new young people with talent and eager to learn.

Ynyshir Band with their conductor, Fred Nicholas, at Ebbw Vale in 1995.

Ladies of Railway Terrace, Ynyshir organising a street party to celebrate the coronation of Queen Elizabeth II in 1953.

'Loco' passing through Ynyshir on its way to Maerdy Colliery to bring down the last coal train, 31 July 1986.

Wattstown halt and goods-yard, about the turn of the century.

Evan, Wilfred and Les Jones, No. 7 Bryn
Terrace, Wattstown, 1922. Little boys
were tucked and when potty trained
they were britched.

Group of children from Bryn Terrace, Wattstown, 1930. Wilfred Jones is first on the left in the
front row.

The Jones family of Wattstown in 1937. Parents: Evan Jones, Eliza Jones. Sons: Evan, Wilfred, Leslie, Stanley, Frederick and Brynmor. Daughter: Betty.

Wattstown AFC, winners of the South Wales and Monmouthshire Junior Cup and Gold Medals, 1924-25. From left to right, back row: E. Potter, L. Davies, T. Rees (President), S. Harris, W. Jones, G. Owen. Middle row: E. Durbin, E. Vaughan, W. Harris, G. Griffiths, E. Hammond, Sam Howells, R. Gunter (Vice-Captain), D. Radcliffe, W.G. Kent (Trainer), T. Bowen, (Vice-President). Seated, front row: C. Benbow, G. Hemmings, T. Thomas, E. Thomas, Councillor John Kane ME, JP (President), Sim. Howells (Captain), Ivor Thomas, D.J. Latham (Financial Secretary), G.R. John (General Secretary). Cross-legged on ground: R. O'Neil, P. Jenkins.

Wattstown Boys Club, winners of the first Welsh Basketball Championship Basketball, 1936.

Pigeon fanciers, Wattstown, c. 1930. From left to right: Randy Stroud, Joe Morgan, Fred Rees and Dai Rowlands.

Scene at Wattstown Colliery on the day of the disaster. At 11.45 a.m., Tuesday, 11 July 1905 an explosion, resulting in appalling loss of life, occurred at the National Colliery, Wattstown. At the time of the explosion 930 persons were employed in the No. 1 Pit which escaped the explosion and 120 persons in the No. 2 Pit. Of these 120, 117 were killed by the violence of the explosion or by the effects of afterdamp. Three survivors were found: John Reeves who lived for six hours after his rescue; John Dando who survived for fifteen hours (both Reeves and Dando had suffered horrendous injuries and died of shock); Matthew Davies, who did recover but was not well enough to give evidence at the inquiry. Of the 119 victims nearly half were under twenty years of age and fourteen were under fourteen years old. The youngest was a thirteen-year-old boy, W.A. Williams of No. 14 School Street, Ynyshir, who died from the effect of afterdamp. The oldest victim was D. Johnson (aged 64), a labourer who died from burns. Also among the dead was the colliery manager, Mr William Meredith, who was originally from the Swansea Valley. He had been in complete control of the colliery since 1898. The cause of the accident was the explosive used to blast through a barrier between the heading and the upcast shaft. Gelignite was technically permitted in the sinking of a pit but was not permissible in a coal mine which contained gas. Gelignite, however, was used to blow away the barrier. Mr Milner Jones reporting to the Secretary of State stated: 'The evidence given at the inquest discloses a total disregard of statutory rules for the use of explosives in a mine where gas had been found. As Mr Meredith, the Manager and Agent, who had entire control of the mine had been killed, prosecution was not recommended.'

On the afternoon of Thursday, 13 July 1905, this message was received from Lord Knollys on behalf of the King, it read: 'To the Manager, Wattstown Colliery, Pontypridd, Wales. The King is anxious to express to you personally, the widows, orphans and other relations of those who have lost their lives in the recent colliery accident, the profound sympathy which he and the Queen entertain for them on the overwhelming calamity which has befallen them. Their Majesties feel most sincerely and deeply for them in their great sorrow.'

84

James Rhys Jones, undertaker, 76 Ynyshir Road, Ynyshir,
who can be seen seated on the hearse (picture below). The
funerals of the victims took place over three days – Friday,
Saturday and Sunday. On the Friday Mr Meredith, the
late manager, and twelve others were interred at Llethrdu
Cemetery, Trealaw, some five miles from Wattstown. A
large gathering of people assembled at Wattstown Bridge
and the funeral procession extended for over a mile and
took twenty-eight minutes to pass over the bridge. The
majority of the bodies were interred on the Saturday at
Llethrdu Cemetery. with the cortege extending for some
five miles. The first part entered the gates of the cemetery
almost before the last part had left Wattstown. Thousands
upon thousands of people lined the route from Wattstown
to Trealaw to witness the sorrowful event. Men and
women openly showed their grief and young children
looked on in bewilderment. The funeral travelled the
route in complete silence apart from the impromptu sound
of an old Welsh hymn rising from the saddened onlookers.
At the same time on the Saturday, five of the victims were
buried at Treorchy Cemetery. One man, Mr William
Thomas John of Ynyshir, was conveyed to Treorchy by a
special train provided by the Taff Vale Railway. His body
was accompanied by the Ynyshir Drum and Fife Band with
which he had been associated. The scene at Treorchy was
the same as that at Trealaw. Thousands of people had
gathered at the cemetery to witness the sad event.

The hearse, bearing the coffin of the colliery manager, Mr William Meredith, Friday, 14 July
1905. The last four victims were interred on Sunday. Another huge procession took place,
no less than that for the preceding days. It was reported that the scene at the gravesides was
'most pathetic, especially when two or even three members of the same family were buried at
the same time.'

'Time for a chat over the garden fence'. A group of miners' wives and children, Wattstown, 1931.

Miner and his family (some of whom are also in the top picture), Wattstown, 1931.

Members of Porth Rhondda Girls Grammar School on a conducted tour of Wattstown Colliery, 1949.

Fitters and maintenance men of Wattstown Colliery pictured here with Mr Sam Thomas (top row, second left) on his retirement in 1957.

Members of National Colliery Lodge (of the National Union of Mineworkers), outside Wattstown Miners Institute, 1959.

National Colliery, Wattstown, on the day of its closure – 22 November 1968.

Three
Pontygwaith, Tylorstown and Stanleytown

Artist's impression of the iron works at Pontygwaith, *c.* 1629. The area is now known as Furnace Road.

General view of Pontygwaith, pre-1909, with Fern Vale Brewery on the right of picture.

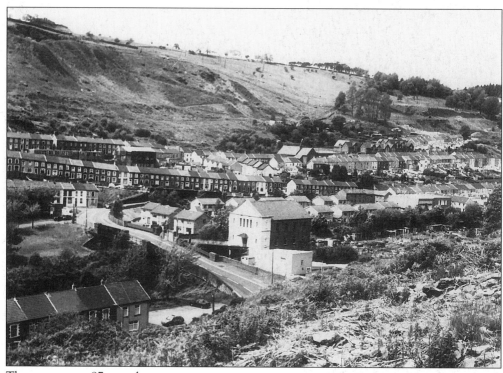

The same scene 87 years later.

Jazz bands parading through Pontygwaith in August 1954.

Stanleytown Infants School, 1901.

The Stanley Hotel, built in 1900 for the Rhondda Valley Breweries. It was the first public house in Stanleytown where, at that time, only the school and three rows of houses existed: Upper Terrace, Middle Terrace and Lower Terrace.

Mr David Thomas with his wife Mary Ann Thomas. They were the first tenants of the Stanley Hotel (1900-1921) and are pictured here in 1900 with their two children Lizzie and Dai. Later, there were to be four more children. To attract trade tavern tokens (see below) were introduced. Initially, there was a skittle alley (demolished c. 1910) at the Stanley and matches were organised with other public houses. The winners were awarded tokens to the value of 3d. 'Smoking concerts' were also held where each performer would be given a token for 'doing his act'. By the First World War it seems that tavern tokens were no longer used as a currency at the Stanley and this was probably one of the last promotional ventures of its kind. In 1982, a token, together with documents and contracts between Mr David Thomas and Rhondda Breweries, were given to the National Museum of Wales, Cardiff (who showed considerable interest) by his last surviving child – Rachel Ann James ('Raddie' Thomas). The last tenant of the Stanley was Mr Cyril 'Sparky' Smith. He was there until the pub burned down on Monday, 26 August 1976.

This is an example of the tavern tokens used by the Stanley Hotel.

Mrs Mary Ann Thomas (seated front, right) with a group of her friends, *c.* 1910. They would gather together after chapel on Sunday nights and have a supper and chat at the Stanley Hotel. Rhondda was 'dry' on a Sunday then as the public houses did not open.

Carnival at Stanleytown in celebration of the coronation of Queen Elizabeth II, 1953.

Fancy dress parade outside the Stanley Hotel, 1953.

Jean Gifford aged 16, of Witherdene Street, Stanleytown, *c.* 1950. The large building in the background is the Stanley Hotel.

Tylorstown Girls' School, *c*. 1903.

Tylorstown Boys' School, 1906.

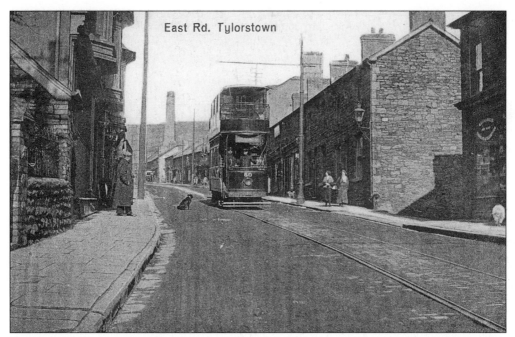

Tram travelling down from Ferndale along East Road, Tylorstown, *c.* 1910. The stack visible is from the Pendyrus Colliery, Tylorstown.

Tylorstown Ambulance Division displaying their trophies, 1917.

Tylorstown Harriers Athletic Club, 1937.

Tylorstown railway station, c. 1922, looking south down the valley towards Porth.

The sinking of No. 9 pit Tylorstown in 1907. The bricks piled up were to be used for lining the shaft. The first two shafts in Tylorstown were sunk by Alfred Tylor in 1873. The colliery was officially called Pendyrus Colliery, but came to be known as Tylor's thus giving the name of Tylorstown to the village. The colliery was purchased by David Davis of Ferndale in 1894 and given the numbers of 6 and 7. An earlier pit known as Cynllwyn-Du, sunk by Thomas Wayne in 1858 at Pontygwaith was also purchased by David Davis, but remained closed until 1892 when the shaft was deepened and then given the number 8. David Davis sunk No. 9 himself in 1907. This was the last pit in Tylorstown to work coal; it closed in 1960. Nos 6 and 7 ceased coaling in the early 1930s and No. 8 in 1935.

Tylorstown Colliery power station which was destroyed by fire in 1924.

General view of Tylorstown Collieries, 1920s.

'Local Boy Makes Good'. Gwilym Cynlais Thomas and wife Ruby, formerly of 34 Parry Street, Tylorstown, who became Mayor and Mayoress of Nuneaton, Warwickshire.

Pendyrus Choir at Tylorstown in 1928 with conductor, Mr Arthur Duggan. In May 1924 a group of young miners, led by Emlyn Drew and Ben Jones, met in the Miners' Federation room at Tylorstown to discus the feasibility of forming a 'Male Voice Choir'. Choral music had begun in the Rhondda Valleys some seventy years earlier, and there were already several famous male choirs in the area – so why not one in the upper Rhondda Fach? The first auditions of choristers were held in the vestry of Ebenezer chapel, Tylorstown, and the first committee meeting took place in the Miners' Federation room on 24 May 1924 – henceforth the 'official birthday' of the choir. A name was required. Old maps of the area showed the existence of two farms – Pendyrus Uchaf and Pendyrus Isaf – on the slopes leading up to Llanwynno. It is conceivable that the new choir might have been called 'Tylorstown', but Pendyrus seemed more historical and more romantic, and was adopted instead. Pendyrus Choir soon outgrew Ebenezer vestry, and rehearsals were moved to the junior school in Edmund Street, which remains the choir's base over seventy years later.

The Pendyrus Male Choir conducted by Arthur Duggan which won first prize at the National Eisteddfod of Wales, held at Caernarfon in 1935. The pre-war years were times of mass unemployment and poverty in the valleys, and the choir's concert activities were devoted to raising funds for a variety of charitable causes. This work was much appreciated, as were the choir's radio broadcasts, and ensured local support for the choir in its ventures on the eisteddfod platform – both in Rhondda and nationally. By 1939 work in the mines had become increasingly scarce, and of the choir's singing strength of 153 men, sixty per cent were unemployed. Currently there are but a few retired miners on the register, the last 'collier/chorister' having left the industry at the closure of Maerdy Colliery in 1990. Pendyrus Choir presented fifty-one consecutive annual concerts at Ferndale Workmen's Hall – the first in 1927. These 'annuals' were discontinued after the 51st (in 1978), but revived in 1982. In latter years these concerts had been held in November, but because of heating problems at the Hall, the venue was moved to Trerhondda chapel, Ferndale in 1983. The choir held its last

'annual' at the Workmen's Hall in 1984, and made only one further appearance there, in the 'Mabon's Day' celebration in 1986. Ferndale Workmen's Hall had by then become very dilapidated, and was eventually demolished in January 1995. Pendyrus can boast of having had only three conductors in its seventy-two year history. Arthur Duggan, awarded the MBE for his services to music in Wales in 1954, was the first and he was followed by the two-year conductorship of Glan Lewis (the choir's former accompanist). In 1962 the choir's present Musical Director was appointed. A music teacher in his home town, Merthyr Tydfil, Glynne Jones went on to become Senior Music Advisor for Gwent, involving himself, for 25 years, in all aspects of music-making among young people in that county. He has put his wide musical experience at the disposal of Pendyrus, and has enhanced the choir's reputation immeasurably. His contribution to music in schools and the community at large has been recognised by a Fellowship at the Welsh College of Music and Drama, and, like his predecessor, by the award of the MBE in the 1996 Honours List.

Pendyrus Male Choir, during their Canadian tour, September 1965. The choir's reputation has spread throughout the British Isles, and beyond. It frequently appears in concerts and festivals, and on television, in Wales and England, and has toured in Scotland and Northern Ireland. Pendyrus has performed in Brussels, Moscow and St Petersburg, and has made an extensive three-week tour of Australia (including appearances at international festivals of Perth, Sydney and Melbourne), three visits to Canada, and six tours in the United States. To mark Pendyrus' Golden Jubilee in 1974 the choir received the Rhondda Recognition Award, and was entertained to dinner by the Mayor and councillors of the Borough of Rhondda.

Pendyrus Choir at Oundle College, 17 July 1993. The choir's current membership encompasses men drawn from all walks of life, and from a wide area of South Wales, but all are agreed that there is no question of Pendyrus moving from its birthplace. It will always be an ambassador for Rhondda Fach.

Four
Ferndale and Maerdy

Ferndale Prize Band, *c.* 1880.

School mistresses, Ferndale, *c.* 1895. The older girls were used as teachers' help to look after the younger children.

Skating on the lake at Darran Park, Ferndale, frozen solid in 1905.

Schoolboys at the Strand, Ferndale, *c.* 1900.

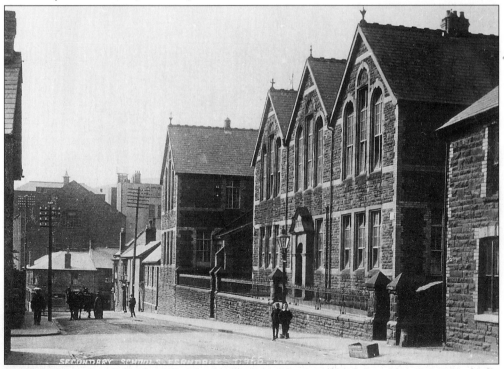

Ferndale Secondary School, 1900. This building was destroyed by fire and has now completely disappeared.

Ferndale Fire Brigade, c. 1905.

The first tram at Ferndale, 1908.

Artists impression of the Ferndale Colliery disaster, 8 November 1867. The explosion was caused by men working in conditions of gas with naked lights and resulted in the death of 178 men and boys. Thomas Powell, a lamp-keeper, said at the inquiry that he had suspected for some time that the lamps had been tampered with and had reported this to the manager, Mr Williams, who had replied, 'I don't know what to do, they are a rough lot'. The conclusion of the jury stated that the cause of the explosion was an accumulation of gas in the workings being fired by a number of men illegally removing the top off the safety lamps, to gain more light. Several lamps were found to be tampered with and keys for opening the lamps were found in the pockets of some of the bodies. On 10 June 1869 a second explosion occurred at Ferndale killing fifty-three men and boys. Again the cause of this explosion was the illegal opening of safety lamps.

Officials and police sergeant, Ferndale Colliery, 1897.

Ferndale Colliery's pay office (left), *c.* 1900. Centre background is the Salisbury Hotel, now headquarters of Ferndale Rugby Club.

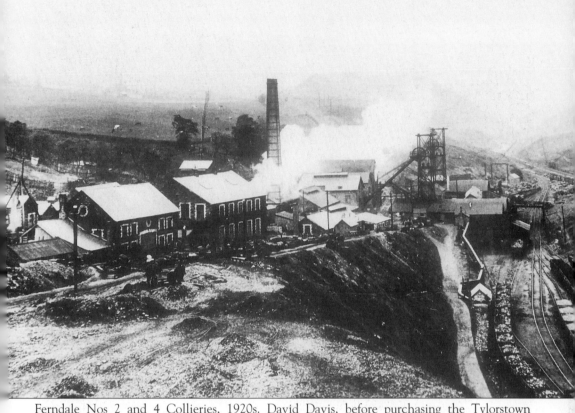

Ferndale Nos 2 and 4 Collieries, 1920s. David Davis, before purchasing the Tylorstown collieries, sunk four pits in Ferndale: No. 1 in 1861, No. 2 in 1870, No. 4 in 1876 and No. 5 in 1889. The missing No. 3 was the Bodringallt Colliery sunk in 1864 at Ystrad, Rhondda Fawr on the other side of the mountain from Ferndale. The Nos 2 and 4 pits closed in the late 1930s, Nos 1 and 5 worked up until 1959 with No. 3 kept open as an 'air pit' for ventilation.

Jazz band competition at Ferndale during the Miners' Strike, 1926.

Float advertising Victoria animal and pet foods, Ferndale, 1926.

Striking miners building a culvert at Ferndale, 1926.

'Self-help group'. This group of miners became shoe makers and repairers during the strike of 1926.

Soup kitchens, Ferndale, 1926.

Children eagerly waiting for their free meal at their school in Ferndale during the Miners' Strike, 1926.

The opening of the Ferndale branch of the Co-operative Society in 1935.

Standard 1 at Ferndale School in 1929, pictured on the mountain-side behind the school.

Ferndale School football team, champions of Glamorgan, 1954-55 season.

General view of Ferndale, mid-1950s.

Assembly Rooms on fire at Blaenllechau, *c.* 1902.

Ferndale Swimming Baths, 1940s.

Morlais Male Choir pictured at their headquarters, Ferndale. In 1927, Mr Alfred J. Morgan and twelve of his friends formed a glee group, calling themselves the Mustard Club. This was the forerunner of the Morlais Choir. Their first effort at competition was at Hermon chapel, Pontygwaith, where they took first place. They next competed at Salem chapel, Ferndale, again winning first prize. It was then decided to draw up a constitution and elect a committee and the Morlais was officially born. The choir's first major success was at Pontypridd Eisteddfod on the 7 February 1929 where they beat five other choirs. Over the next four decades the choir went from strength to strength appearing and completing all over Wales, even making two appearances at Cardiff Prison. 1963 was another landmark for the choir – their Easter tour of Baden-Württemberg, Germany. This was the first of many overseas trips they were to make. Most recently (July 1996) the choir toured North America where they were given a tremendous reception.

Main road in Maerdy looking toward Ferndale, 1908. On the top right of the photograph is
Maerdy Cemetery.

Main road, Maerdy looking north, before the days of the trams, c. 1900.

Mr Francome and Mr Tom Jones being presented with a bowls trophy by Mr A.C.F. Evans, 1948. In the background can be seen the by-then disused Maerdy Nos 1 and 2 pits.

Opening of Ebenezer chapel, Maerdy, 1912.

Memorial situated in the grounds of Maerdy church dedicated to the Maerdy Colliery disaster, 1885.

DEDICATED
TO THE MEMORY OF
THOSE 81 MEN KILLED AT
MARDY COLLIERY DISASTER
24TH DECEMBER 1885
BY THE MOST REVEREND
D G CHILDS
LORD ARCHBISHOP OF WALES
30TH JUNE 1985
IN THE PRESENCE OF
CLLR GLYN JAMES
MAYOR OF RHONDDA

Maerdy Colliery after the modernisation programme of 1958.

Maerdy Colliery in full production a few years before its closure. The first pits at Maerdy, known as No. 1 and No. 2, were sunk by two men from Brecon – Mr Mordecai Jones and Mr Wheatly Cobb, raising coal in 1876. The following year, however, the colliery was acquired by the Locketts Merthyr Company. On Christmas Eve, 1885, an explosion took place killing eighty-one men and boys, the explosion probably being caused by a flame igniting firedamp. A medal for bravery was awarded to Mr William Thomas, manager, for the part he played in leading the rescue operation. Locketts sunk two more pits in Maerdy (No. 3 in 1893 and No. 4 in 1914) about a mile north of Nos 1 and 2. These two new pits were used as an upcast shaft and to bring coal up from the older Nos 1 and 2 pits. In 1932, Locketts sold up to the Welsh Associated Collieries who ran the Nos 3 and 4 pits until 1934 when the concern passed into the hands of Powell Dyffryn Associated Collieries Limited who worked Maerdy until 1940 when production was suspended due to lack of demand. From 1940 until nationalisation in 1947, barely enough coal was raised to sustain the colliery. In 1948, however, the National Coal Board (NCB) approved a £5 million modernisation programme. At this time an underground road was cut to Bwllfa No. 1 in the Aberdare Valley which was to be used for ventilation. In 1957, Bwllfa No. 2 was closed and the workforce transferred to Maerdy. By 1958 the modernisation programme had been fully completed and a promise of a hundred years of work was given by the NCB. In 1985, it was linked to Tower Colliery, Hirwaun but five years later on 21 December 1990 Maerdy Colliery closed with the loss of 750 jobs. A long way short of the hundred years promised. Tower Colliery, the last deep mine still operating in South Wales, was eventually bought by a workers' consortium who are currently making a tremendous success of the business.

122

One of the last group of miners to return to the surface on the day Maerdy closed, 21 December 1990.

March away from the colliery after closing ceremony. The procession was led by Allan Rogers MP and Annie Powell, Mayoress of Rhondda.

The dismantling of Maerdy Colliery, February 1991.

Maerdy Colliery during its dismantling.

A desolate scene. Maerdy Colliery is no more. The end of 125 years of coal production.

'Sally, Sally, the horse that saved the valley'. On a December day in 1969 a major disaster was averted (the flooding of the Rhondda Fach) when a fault was found in the retaining bank of the Lluest Wen dam, two miles above Maerdy. The song, Sali (Sally) Lluest Wen (reproduced on the following page), was composed by Hawys and Glyn James and tells the story of that day. Pictured above, with Sally the black mare and her rider Lyn, are the girls who won first prize at the Urdd Eisteddfod singing the ballad.

SALI (SALLY) LLUEST WEN

doh **D** Llon/Major Bywiog/Briskly

Rhyw ddeu - ddydd cyn Nad - ol - ig, Ym mil naw chwe deg naw, Roedd
One wet day in De - cem - ber, In nine - teen six - ty nine, A

llanc ar ge - fen ca - seg Yn crwy - dro yn y glaw. A chwil - io roedd am
youth called Lyn was ri - ding Two miles from Maer - dy mine. For lost sheep he was

dde - faid Ger - llaw hen gron - fa ddŵr A Sa - li oedd y ga - a - seg a
sear - ching A - long the hill - sides bare Near Llu - est Wen's deep wa - a - ters on

Lyn oedd en - w'r gw - w - wr. **Cytgan/Chorus** Sa - li, Sa - li, S'dim rhaid i neb ddy-
Sall - y his black ma - a - are. Sa - lly, Sa - lly, The horse that saved the

fa - lu Hon heb os nac on - i - bai Ach - u - bodd Y Rhon - dda
va - lley She de - serves a song of praise For sa - ving the Rhon - dda

Fach_ Y Rhon_dda Fach.
Fach_ Y Rhon_dda Fach.

---

2 Wrth groesi crib yr argae
Yn ddedwydd ar ei hynt
A phedair coes y gaseg
Ar garlam yn y gwynt,
Yn sydyn heb un rhybudd
Agorodd 'dani dwll,
A syrthio wnaeth y gaseg
Yn ddwfn i lawr i'r pwll.

3 A Lyn a redodd ymaith
A'i gorff yn wlyb gan chwys,
I lawr i ben pwll Maerdy
I geisio cymorth brys,
Ac yna 'mhen rhyw 'chydig
Y frigâd dân a ddaeth
A chodwyd Sali 'fyny
O'r pwll lle'r oedd mor gaeth.

4 A hyn a roddodd rybudd
Fod peryg i'r holl ddwr
I dorri drwy'r hen argae
A boddi'r cwm bid siwr,
Y glewion ddaeth i'r adwy
I g'wiro'r Lluest Wen,
A diolch rown i Sali
Clodforwn hi yn ben.

---

2 As Lyn and Sally hastened
Upon their homeward way,
Across the dam they galloped
That wet and wintry day,
Quite suddenly below them
A deep hole like a well
Appeared without a warning—
And down it Sally fell.

3 Then Lyn was really worried
And fear filled his mind,
He ran to Maerdy pit-top
For help he had to find,
Quite soon with bells a-ringing
The fire brigade came there,
They worked so hard to rescue
And free the poor, black mare.

4 So Sally's fall gave warning
That danger was at hand,
For soon the dam would fracture
And water flood the land,
Men rushed from all directions
The old dam to repair,
Our thanks we'll give to Sally,
Let's praise that great black mare

End of an era

How oh valley green and quiet
frightful then the secret diet
that vile evil thou didst wreak
upon poor man so small and meek.

Your torture took the form of dust
& was their sad ending right or Just
vengeful spite you had in store
in aged youth they coughed no more.

They welcomed death with heaving chest
so grateful for that timeless rest
mining men of middle age
were called to death by coal dust rage.

In graveyards bleak the white stones stand
most are humble, a few are grand
but they tell the story stark
of those who died within the dark.

They didnt go below by greed
but sweated there for simple need
gravestones in that sacred place
now stand like stubble on thy face.

The owners reaped and then didst flee
without a further thought for thee
and travelled to another place
some further nature to debase.

Your hilltops are much greener now
& gone are the tips that marked thy brow
river beds are once more clean
amongst all vales you stand supreme.

So let the folk in future time
whilst on your mountains carefree climb
not forget that time of shame
but speak in awe of rhondda's fame.

Haydn Rees

'End of an Era', poem by Haydn Rees.

Three retired miners, Glyn Harries, Bryn Rees and Idris Jenkins, reflect on their working days in the collieries that have now disappeared, 1984.

Acknowledgements

The authors wish to express their thanks and gratitude to the following
for their co-operation in the compiling of this book.
Sarah Morgan for her work with the computer; Margaret Rudd; Ivor Palmey;
Malcolm Jones; John H. Lewis (Secretary of Pendyrus Choir) for contributing much valuble
information about the choir's history; Derek Andrews (Ynyshir Band); Rachel Rowe;
Des Phelps; Kenneth Haynes; Adelina Evans (for her translation of Welsh to English);
Alan Phillips; Dilwyn Evans (for sharing his vivid memories of Porth with us); Maureen Bents;
Phil Caddy, Norman Carter, Wilfred Jones; Gwyn Harries; Percy Kingsbury; John Nagle;
Keith Edmunds; Gerry Lynch; John Williams; Emlyn Bibey; Tydfil Breeze; Roy Thomas;
Bert Diambro; Treorchy Library; Lilian Evans; Mary Vignali; Brian Davies;
Hawys and Glyn James; Elfed Evans; Ray Wiltshire; Haydn Farnham, Emlyn Cameron.
Apologies to anyone else who we have failed to mention.
P.S. The authors would be delighted to hear from anybody who wishes to loan for copying old
photographs that have not already been published.
These may well find their way into volume two. Please contact:
Glyn Rudd (Tel: 01443 685674)
Aldo Bacchetta c/o 2-4 Station Street, Porth, CF39 9NR (Tel: 01443 682256)